WOW

Crystal Grey

BALBOA.
PRESS

A DIVISION OF HAY HOUSE

Balboa Press books may be ordered through booksellers or by contacting:

Balboa Press
A Division of Hay House
1663 Liberty Drive
Bloomington, IN 47403
www.balboapress.com
1 (877) 407-4847

Because of the dynamic nature of the Internet, any web addresses or links contained in this book may have changed since publication and may no longer be valid. The views expressed in this work are solely those of the author and do not necessarily reflect the views of the publisher, and the publisher hereby disclaims any responsibility for them.

The author of this book does not dispense medical advice or prescribe the use of any technique as a form of treatment for physical, emotional, or medical problems without the advice of a physician, either directly or indirectly. The intent of the author is only to offer information of a general nature to help you in your quest for emotional and spiritual well-being. In the event you use any of the information in this book for yourself, which is your constitutional right, the author and the publisher assume no responsibility for your actions.

Any people depicted in stock imagery provided by Thinkstock are models, and such images are being used for illustrative purposes only. Certain stock imagery © Thinkstock.

Printed in the United States of America.

ISBN: 978-1-4525-9918-2 (sc)
ISBN: 978-1-4525-9919-9 (e)

Balboa Press rev. date: 11/17/2014

ANGEL EYES.......

12/31/2013

Shed no tears, mourn no more.
With My Wings, I Now Soar.
Way up High in the sky.
With GOD'S GRACE, I Can FLY.
I'm On Earth 2, In desquise.
In the depths, Of ANGELS EYES.......

AMERICAN BLEND....

I am a American Blend..... of many different paths.

A mixture of many, thru a Lifetime of laughs.

A little bit of this a little bit of that.

Thankful I am....4 Freedom is where it's at.

Some will ask, exactly what nationality or religion are U.

I smile and laugh, knowing that the American Blend, is a clue.

My roots run deep and have scattered across the many seas.

4 the Life I have Lived was touched by many, in the Living breeze.

I am not One but many, and Endless are those

whom made a difference per say.

and my mixture is of many,, part this and that, made from American clay.

I had Freedom 2 read any book, of wit, 2 study and vote.

I could even run a business or own Land and boat.

My blood is so many different types, as well as my religion.

I choose not 2 compare or compete, a personal decision.

Some say I am nothing unless I choose.

And I 4-give them, 4 that's a path, where many do loose.

My blood runs deep and Free, and I have attended many a place.

And I must say, out loud, cool is the Right 2

choose, thru-out Time and Space.

My features are different, and can't really say, I am just one of One.

4 2 me being a American Blend it's what makes

Freedom,individual and Fun.

Some will say you must choose or you really will never belong.

I PRAY 4 their Souls Hearts and Minds..... 4 they got it all, wrong.

One Blood, of LOVE, GOD spoke of how many sands were there.

As well as the Stars that shine, the number,

Infinity, now that's a Eternal layer.

I have witnessed many argue non-stop about this and that.

Understanding not that the American Blend

& Many A Blend is where it's at.

I don't have chose One 2 be considered Special in GOD"S Eyes.

4 I was taught being Humble is a Love 4 All.....

where the Spirit of Gratitude flies.

One Blood of many, with many roots and limbs, that blow in the breeze.

Without comparing and competing, I find

that being Humble is being at ease.

I have witnessed faces turn red as their, blood does boil.

Over the comparison of peoples, like Water and oil.

It doesn't mix well and never will when any compare.

4 pride is not a Tool of Unity but a separating snare.

U may not agree and that's kinds cool, 2.

4 I am an American Blend, and Individuality, is the dew.

I Believe, in Peace and Love, Sharing and Caring.

Education and Wit....4 there's no growth in comparing.

Some will Never understand that's it's cool 2 Unite As Just One.

On Earth as in Heaven, Freedom and Liberty Shall Be Done !

Sometimes I walk away, when people, bicker and compare.

I choose not 2 get involved, 4 that's being Humble Aware.

THE ROOM 2 BLOOM....

The buds were different from their conception.
Lacking the Vibrance of Sturdy Protection.
Some were mishapen others stunted & weak.
For Thousands Of years they grew close 2 the creek.
Without many leaves they could Obsorb All Sound.
As the Skies Parted & Brillant Colors Touched the Ground.
Thru The Laughter Of Angels They Heard A Calm Voice.
As A Whisper In The Wind, 4 A Reason 2 Rejoice.
Reach Out With Your Branches Set your Sights High.
4 Nourishment Within, That Reaches The The Sky.
As The Roots Started Growing Brillant Blossoms Were Fed.
Filling The Forest Floor With Shimmering Blossoms That Spread.
Many Tiny Little Buds Waiting Patiently 2 Bloom.
Once The Path Was Cleared & They Had The Room.
As The Skies Of Heaven Opened 4 those Weak & Slighted.
Many Doors Began 2 Open 4 Ancient Paths, Well Lighted.
GOD-Work In Action As The Skies Parted Once Again.
A Calming Voice Could Be Heard Drifting In The Wind.
No Matter Your Circumstances View As Miracles In Action.
4 The True Path Of Enlightenment & Peaceful Satisfaction.
From The Tinest Plant 2 The Poor Families Forced Away.
GOD'S Will Shall Be Done....4 Peace On Earth, Here 2 Stay !

A F I S H H H A FRIEND IN SPIRIT HAPPY HUMBLE HELPER ...

A MOTHERS EYES....

A Mothers Eyes Just 4 Me.
Preciuos Momoments Thes Eyes Did See.
A First Little Smile On A Body Soo Small.
I Am Still In Wonder Still In Awe.
A First Step Forward Another Step Back.
I Am Still Learning A Humble Honest Fact.
Memories That Nourish Unconidiional Love In The Heart.
Gazing Into The Eyes, Of The Child I Helped Start.
Those Toddler Years, The First Step On A Bus.
It Was So Difficult Allowing It 2 not Be Just Us.
There Were Tears In My Eyes, As the Bus Pulled Away.
The Emptiness I Felt Words Can Not say.
Legs So Small They Could Barely Reach The Steps.
I Have Done My Very Best With Only A Few Regrets.
No Instructional Manual Came With GOD'S Gift.
The Ones That Changes My Life, Giving Destiny A Lift.
I Didn't Really Have Others 2 Assist With The Care.
Much They Missed Out On Up Memory's Fond Stair.
Those Teenage Years With Katie Kaboom.
When I Drift Back Now Laughter Fills the Room.
Those Phone Calls & Tears Between The Children & I.
Loving Links Of Loyalty As The Years Were Passin By.
Their Honesty & Opinions That Come Straight From The Heart.
Between These Children & I....Blesisons From The Start.

Thru The Valley Of Life, Young Children Now Grown.
I Thank GOD Everyday....4 The Love We Have Known !

A Rippling Of Echoes, Whispering At Night.
GOD-Work In Action, As Angels Take Flight.
A Whisper In The Wind, Sent From Above.
Full Of Grace Glory & Love.
Tucked Within, Where Faith Does Reside.
Seek 2 Welcome Humbleness, loose the pride.
Miracles In Action, A Rainbow A Dove.
The Rippling Effect.... Of Spiritual Love !

ANCIENT....

Ancient I Am, Ancient & Old.
Dwelling Within the Shy & the Bold.
Whisper I Do, Whisper In Your Ear.
Words Of Peace Perfectly Clear.
Food I Am Food 4 The Soul.
Nourishment 4 The Body As A Whole.
Caressing I Am, Caressing To The Mind.
Tucked Within, Wisdom 4 The blind.
Always I Am, Always I Am Here.
Waiting 2 Bloom, 4 Faith 2 Appear.
Lonely I Was Lonely 2 Be Me.
Waiting Many Lifetimes, To Finally Be Free.
When I Am Nourished, U Shall Know.
As Your Soul....Begins 2 Grow !

EXPRESSIONS....

01-17-2006

A form of expression 2 Heal Inner pain.

A splash Of Sunshine A drop of rain.

At Times no Words Spoken or tossed In the Air.

A Dab Of Artwork Ones Able To Share.

Art from the Soul stealing The Show.

Used 2 Express 4 Creativety 2 Flow.

Or Words Of Comfort, Words That ryme.

Art In Many Forms Thru-out All space & Time.

A Very First project Of Clouds In the sky.

Displayed On The wall as others walk by.

Used 4 many Centuries 2 Teach & 4 Healing.

Full Of Emotion If Strokes Or Words have Feeling.

4 Children Its A Must Expressions In Print.

2 Nourish Lifetimes Of Time well spent.

Frozen In Time A Work Of Art.

A Guide 4 All With A Expressive Start.

2 A Image of devastation after a hurricane.

A Rippling Of Silence Yet Art Heals The pain.

Some say its not a need yet the really don't know.

How One Expressive Picture, Can Help Another Grow.

Art 4 The Mind, Art 4 The Soul.

Can Nourish The Body, As A Whole !

HAPPY DOG....

It All Started With Me Time A Short Trip 4 Meditation.
Into The Beauty Of Nature, Full Of Wonder & Inspiration.
As I Was Driving Along A Black & White Dog Appeared.
As I Hit The Brakes 2 See If The Path Ahead Looked Cleared.
Then I Saw The Dog Rolling In The Weeds As Though He's Been Hit.
As I Opened My Car Door In A Flash That Dog Did Sit.
He Had Jumped Over My Lap Into The Passenger Seat.
In Entered A Dog On A Mission, That Loved 2 Greet.
I Requested He Get Out & He Looked At Me Kinda Sad.
So On My Mission I Went, Beside A Dog That Looked Glad !
When I Got Back 2 The House My Oldest Ran Out.
2 See What All That Barking & Screeching Was About.
Out Of Nowhere The Pet Cat Had Spotted The Dog.
& Pounceded On His Back, Being A territorail Hog.
So We Brought Him Inside Cleaned Up The Bloody Mess.
Now We Had A Happy Dog Living At The Address.
Meanwhile He Became The Designated Bus Greeter On Call.
He Bonded Instantly With My Youngest, As A Angel On Call.
We Took Him 2 The Local Vets & Animal Shelter's Crew.
Asking If Anyone Knew Who The Dog Belonged 2.
The Lady At The Shelter Smiled & Said With A Happy Grin.
Look At His Doggy Smile, Hes Got A New Place 2 Begin.
One Week Later A Lady Called Claiming To Be The Dogs Owner.

Halfway Back 2 Her House He Jumped Out
& Was Back,Happy 2 Be A Loaner.
She Accepted Finacially Responsibilty I Took
Physical, There was Visitation Rights 2.
A Dog On A Mission 2 Cheer Some Girls Once sad & blue.
HIs Name Was Holstein, He Was Spotted Like A Cow.
We Named Him Lucky, That Was His Name 4 Now.
When We Moved 2 Another State Even The Cops Knew The Dogs Name.
He Would Appear In A Time Of Need Lucky
Dog Had Earned Local Fame.
By Doing What Dogs Do Being A Loyal Friend & Protector 2.
Now A Happy Dog On A Mission Grateful 2 Be Part Of The Crew !

IN THE FAMILIES CUP....
& BOTH NEED PROOFED
POWER OF LOVE, ON
EARTH AS ABOVE....

They Defended Kindness & Their Mom & Their Dad 2.

Then The courts intervened & that relationship was thru.

Adding more poverty friction & fee fine separation.

By not Welcoming Or Promoting Friendship & Parental Obligation.

Forcing the Kin 2 Chose from states not working together.

Causing more family Foundations 2 crumble, from lack of Unitys Tether.

The Court systems had unknowingly ripped many Families Apart.

And made sure that hadn't the funds 4 a New Start !

Interferinng with Parental Peacemaking so the Children Could See.

How not 2 handle inner conflicts that only added to more poverty.

Then more laws were added locking Many Of The Dads & Moms Up.

Instead Of Empowering Taking All the proceeds from The Families Cup !

Suffering 2 Establish How Gov arent to act by adding incarceration.

Instead Seeking 2 Empower & Enlighten With Resources & Education.

Instead of taking away wages & incomes & Many A InHeritences 2.

All Parts Of A Nations Gov Are 2 Empower Than

Allow FREEDOM 2 SHINE THRU.

Freedom Means Choices More Than One In Order 2 Grow.

Thats All Truth 2 Living Light All Nations Need 2 Know !

Health Insurance Is A Needed Wage 2, 4 Inner Fruitfull Security.
As Well As Karing 4 The Elders Sickly, 4 Wisdom Of Honor & Purity.
Amazing Shall Be The Miracles In Action Universal 4 One & All.
When Nations Are Wise & Humble Enough 2 Welcome GOD-Given Law.
4 Peace 2 Flow & Wages & Resources 2 Grow.
Seek 2 Honor GODLY GUIDANCE 4 ALL Proceeds Of Reap Sow.

RESPECT & PROTECT....

Teach Them Right 4 All Respect.
& Thats Honor 2 Protect.
Serve Love A Dash Of Compassion 2.
4 Peace & Love.... 2 Get Thru.
Heap Lots If Dignity & Humble Pie.
4 Passion Of Purpose 2 Really Fly.
Add A Dash Of Empowerment & Fruitfull Wages.
4 Freedom In Actions Many Stages.
toss neglect, silence & ignorance 2.
4 All Truth, 2 Really Shine Thru.
seek not 2 be a sneaker or peeker.
Seek 2 Be A Speaker & A Seeker.
learned behavior, violence abuse & neglect.
Teach Them Right.... 4 Love 2 Protect.
no matter income, heritage, religion or gender.
Always Seek 2 Be A Peaceful Defender.
Heaping Coals Of Kindness & Compassion.
4 Peace In Action Always In Fashion.
Seeking 2 Make The World A Better Place.
Starts With Serving Kindness 2 The Human Race.
suffering 2 Establish Is A Priveldge InDeed.
& How One Applys Those Lessons 4 Future Feed.
Seek 2 View As Blesisons In Desquise.
4 A Clear Path 4 Happy Humble Wise.
Nourish The Roots Of The Best Point Of View.
4 A Attitude Of Gratitude 2 Really Shine Thru.

THE ROOM 2 BLOOM....

The buds were different from their conception.

Lacking the Vibrance of Sturdy Protection.

Some were mishapen others stunted & weak.

For Thousands Of years they grew close 2 the creek.

Without many leaves they could Obsorb All Sound.

As the Skies Parted & Brillant Colors Touched the Ground.

Thru The Laughter Of Angels They Heard A Calm Voice.

As A Whisper In The Wind, 4 A Reason 2 Rejoice.

Reach Out With Your Branches Set your Sights High.

4 Nourishment Within, That Reaches The The Sky.

As The Roots Started Growing Brillant Blossoms Were Fed.

Filling The Forest Floor With Shimmering Blossoms That Spread.

Many Tiny Little Buds Waiting Patiently 2 Bloom.

Once The Path Was Cleared & They Had The Room.

As The Skies Of Heaven Opened 4 those Weak & Slighted.

Many Doors Began 2 Open 4 Ancient Paths, Well Lighted.

GOD-Work In Action As The Skies Parted Once Again.

A Calming Voice Could Be Heard Drifting In The Wind.

No Matter Your Circumstances View As Miracles In Action.

4 The True Path Of Enlightenment & Peaceful Satisfaction.

From The Tinest Plant 2 The Poor Families Forced Away.

GOD'S Will Shall Be Done....4 Peace On Earth, Here 2 Stay !

The White Wolf Appeared at Times When All Seemed lost.

At Times In Solid Form, & Other Times A Shimmering Frost.

Thru The Dark Nights The Angel Dog Would Twinkle Glisten & Glow.

Other Times It Would Appear 4 Rescues & Show You Where 2 Go.

I Had A Good Friend That was beatin badly & buried alive.

Kidnapped & Raped Missing 4 days With a Will 2 Survive.

That Angel Dog Appeared & Led The Sister 2 The freshly dug grave.

She was lifeless and limp stuck in a catatonic cave.

The Power Of Love & A Sisterly Bond Of Love Soo Pure.

As Well As A White Glowing Wolf Dog Sent By GOD 4 Sure.

Many said they was no hope as Her Sister lay lifeless In Bed.

Yet That Sister refused 2 Give Up, & Prayed & Prayed Instead !

naysayers and doubters weren't allowed in the Room.

Only Good Energy Was Welcomed 4 A Loving Rebirth 2 Bloom.

She Came Out Of The catanoic state after 5 days time.

She was a little slow & recalled not much of the brutal crime.

& With Many Witnesses That Angelic White Wolf Dog Oh Soo Pure.

Finally left The Room & Passed Right Thru The Closed Door !

With The Seed Of Faith & Miracles & The Power 2 Believe.

There Is Nothing GOD & US Really can not Achieve.

The Power Of Love Is Amazing & Awesome InDeed.

Miracles In Action Thru The Lens Of Kind Actions Feed.

This Is A True Story Of Angelic Earthbound Interaction.

May It Nourish All Souls With A Inner Peace Of Satisfaction.

This True Story Was Difficult 2 Write.... 4 I Was That Girl Buried Alive !

Thankful 2 Share ....The Truth

ABOUT THE POWER OF LOVE & A WILL 2 SURVIVE ....

The Power Of....

The Power Of Hope Nourished & Grown.
Shall Move Mountains That Is Known.
The Power Of Prayer From The Soul.
Shall Part The Seas On A Roll.
The Power Of Faith Pure & True.
Shall Give Rise 2 Miracles, GODLY Glue.
The Power Of Wages 2 Nourish All Roots.
Shall Give Rise 2 Honor Amongst Many Suits.
The Power Of Respect 4 Others Loving Traditions.
Shall Bring 4th Renewal 4 Good GODLY Transitions.
The Power Of Truth Shared With The Living.
Shall Give Rise 2 LAWS Of Love 4 The Giving.
The Power Of Sharing 4 Good Fruit Of Good-Will.
Shall Nourish Many Lives 4 Oppourtunites Skill.
The Power Of Love 4 One & All.
Shall Build Many A Bridge Wide & Tall.
The Power Of Enlightenment & Education.
Shall NourishThirsting 4 Knowledge 4 All Motivation !
The Power Of GOD, On Earth My Many Friends.
Thru The Galaxy Of Glory That Never Really Ends.

The Power Of Humbleness Linking Many Others.
Shall Connect Billions In The Sea Of Sisters & Brothers.

The Power Of Simplicity, w/o a clustercluck of confusion.
Shall Give Rise 2 Motion & The Power Of Good Evolution.
The Power Of GOD-LAW w/o foolish fees & regulations.
Shall Give Rise 2 Love 4 Honor & Moral Obligations.
The Power Of Govs Sowing Loyaltys Seed.
Shall Give Rise 2 Honor In Action A Good Fruitfull Feed.
The Power Of Loyalty & Dignity 4 Honorable Representations.
Shall Arise 4 All Peoples 4 Good News Joy & Jubilations.
The Power Of Loyalty & Love 4 Raising Them Right.
Shall Teach even spoiled adults 4 Humbleness & Ensight.
The Power Of Seeking Unto GOD & Your Nations.
Shall Give Arise 2 Love & Loyaltys Eternal Obligations !
The Power Of Learning 2 Empower & Let Go.
Shall Give Rise 2 Freedom Of Choices 4 Wisdom 2 Flow !
The Power Of Respect 4 Others Ancient PeacemakingTraditions.
Shall Give Rise 2 Renewal & Enlightenment 4 Good Transitions.
The Power Of Seeking 2 Ask & Readily Share Informations.
Shall Give Rise 2 Many Fruitfull Resources 4 All Generations.
The Power Of Gov Seeking 2 Sow Loyaltys Seed.
Is Honor On Action A Good Moral & Fruitfull Feed !

The Power Of Good Fruits Reaped & Sown.
Shall Give Rise 2 All Truth In Action That Is Known.
The Power Of Equalty 4 All Upon Earth.
Shall Nourish Good 4 Worldwide Worth.
The Power Of Mercy & 4-Giveness 2.
Shall Produce "Peace" Thats All True !

The Power Of Kindness In The Sea Of Life.

Shall end all wars, suppression & strife.

The Power Of LAW, Given By GOD.

Shall Part The Skies, 4 A Heavenly Nod.

The Power Of Unity without ego or pride.

Shall Link Billions, Connecting Worldwide.

The Power Of Sharing Fruitfull Information.

Shall Nourish Resouces 4 Every Generation.

The Power Of Patience Purpose & Passion.

Shall Soothe Many Souls With Comfort & Compassion.

The Power Of Learning 4 Universal Careers Of Cheers !

Shall Produce Many Fruits & Gifts 4 Faith over fears.

The Power Of Believing That Miracles Exist.

Shall Give Rise 2 Many More, Angels In The Mist !

The Power Of Towns That Welcome & Thrive.

Shall Nourish Many Wages 4 Fruits 2 Survive.

The Power Of Communties That Empower All.

Shall Give Rise 2 Honor 4 A Welcoming Law.

The Power Of Independence & Tools 2 Seek.

Shall Produce Many Discoveries Words That Speak.

The Power Of Good Purpose, Oh Yes Indeed.

Shall Give Rise 2 Many Gifts A Good GODLY Feed !

The Power Of Prayer & Seeking 2 Wait.

Shall Nourish Humbleness As A Inner Trait.

The Power Of Listening 2 Really Know & Hear.

Shall Nourish All Truth, & Thats Krystal Klear.

The Power Of Freedom & Sharing Wisdom Galore.

Shall Give Rise 2 Opening Many A Closed Door.

The Power Of Liberty 2 Enjoy Many Choices.

Shall Nourish Love As Renewals Rejoices !
The Power Of Faith That Love Never Ends.
Shall Give Rise 2 Good News That Equally Defends.
The Power Of Gratitude & Loving Grace.
Shall Give Rise 2 Miracles....Thru-Out All Time & Space !

I am a ADOVOCATE 4 the MEEK.
4 Their RIGHTS these WORDS I SPEAK.
I am a Warrior, 4 GOD 4 The POOR.
4 PEACE & EQUALTY & HUMANITY 2 SOAR.
With Written WORDS, My weapon of CHOICE.
4 GOD"S GLORY, 4 LOVE 2 REJOICE.
I take not the credit 2 GOD I GIVE GLORY.
4 ALL TRUTH 2 LIGHT The LIVING Story.
4 I am PEACEMAKER, TRUTHSEEKER ALL In ONE.
4 JUSTICE & PEACE On EARTH, 2 BE DONE.
As The HOLY ANGELS, GATHER 4 RIGHTOUS LOVE.
I PRAISE GOD, ON EARTH & The HEAVENS ABOVE.
A ANGEL OF MERCY, A ANGEL, 4 GOOD INTENT.
4 WORDS OF HOLY GLORY TIME WELL SPENT !
A MISSION OF LOVE, 4 ALL 2 UNITE.
4 PEACE ON EARTH.......A HOLY LIGHT.

I am a ADOVOCATE 4 the MEEK.
4 Their RIGHTS these WORDS I SPEAK.
I am a Warrior, 4 GOD 4 The POOR.
4 PEACE & EQUALTY & HUMANITY 2 SOAR.
With Written WORDS, My weapon of CHOICE.
4 GOD"S GLORY, 4 LOVE 2 REJOICE.
I take not the credit 2 GOD I GIVE GLORY.

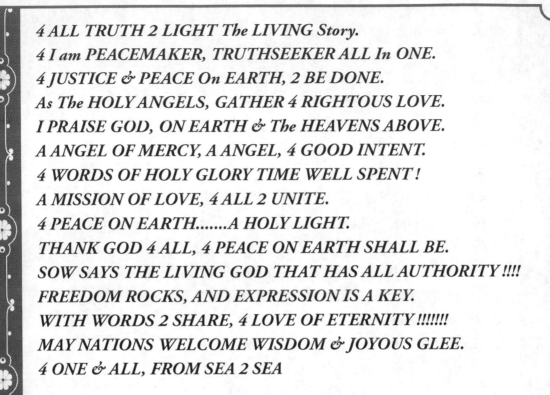

4 ALL TRUTH 2 LIGHT The LIVING Story.

4 I am PEACEMAKER, TRUTHSEEKER ALL In ONE.

4 JUSTICE & PEACE On EARTH, 2 BE DONE.

As The HOLY ANGELS, GATHER 4 RIGHTOUS LOVE.

I PRAISE GOD, ON EARTH & The HEAVENS ABOVE.

A ANGEL OF MERCY, A ANGEL, 4 GOOD INTENT.

4 WORDS OF HOLY GLORY TIME WELL SPENT !

A MISSION OF LOVE, 4 ALL 2 UNITE.

4 PEACE ON EARTH.......A HOLY LIGHT.

THANK GOD 4 ALL, 4 PEACE ON EARTH SHALL BE.

SOW SAYS THE LIVING GOD THAT HAS ALL AUTHORITY !!!!

FREEDOM ROCKS, AND EXPRESSION IS A KEY.

WITH WORDS 2 SHARE, 4 LOVE OF ETERNITY !!!!!!!

MAY NATIONS WELCOME WISDOM & JOYOUS GLEE.

4 ONE & ALL, FROM SEA 2 SEA

FREEDOMS FLOW...

Welcoming Freedom Of Equal Success.
Nourishing Love & Liberty 2 Bless.
What does Freedom mean 2 U.
Allowed Love, 2 Shine Thru.
The Responses Were, Amazing Indeed.
Nourishing Truth, As Social Feed.
Some nations were alittle slow.
& blocked the path, 4 Freedoms Flow.
GOD handled, nations that oppressed.
4 All the Peoples, Freedom Blesssed.
Some Peacemakers weren't Welcomed at all.
Where they nourished not, Freedoms Law.
Eventually those Nations did Learn.
How 2 Seek & How 2 Yearn.
By letting go of ego & pride.
& Welcoming Humbleness, In Lifes Tide.
Wisdom Welcomed & Flowing Indeed.
A Gift From GOD 4 Humble Feed.
When Nations Welcomed GOD 2 Guide.
Gone the ego and the pride.
4 the Light Of Freedoms Glow.
Nourishing Love, 4 All 2 Grow.
Freedom Nourished 4 Gifts & Fruits.
Opened Doors.... On Many Routes.

Responses Were Amazing, Yes Indeed.

Nourishing Truth, As a Social Feed.

Uniting Many Across the Lands.

Freedom Guides, Freedom Stands.

nations let go, of laws that bind.

& Welcomed GOD LAW, Oh Sow Kind.

Nations that were all filled up.

Thirsted 4 GOD Law, In Lifes cup.

without oppression of wealth or gender.

4 GOD is Love & Freedoms Defender!

4 Freedom is, not just a Word.

Welcome Truth & Humbleness Heard.

What does Freedom, mean 2 U.

United Nations, The Living Crew.

Laws Of GOD.... Easy 2 Understand.

Allowed Freedom 2 make A Stand.

& the Living oppressed & suppressed.

Welcomed Freedom.... 2 Be Blessed.

GOD Law GOD Law, Here On Earth.

Welcomed Humbleness.... 4 Freedoms Birth !

ATTITUDE GRATITUDE....

06-9-2014

Every obstacle is a Challenge....With A Thankful Attitude.
Much Can be Accomplished....With Humble Gratitude.
One Of Growth & Clarity....Thru Peaceful Evolution.
4 Contentment Of All....& Honorable Resolution.
Thru The Doorway Of 4-Giveness....Peace Can Really be.
Add A Dash Of Compassion....& Humble Humility.
GOD Gives Us Challenges....2 See If We blame.
Or View it As A Blesison....4 Betterment, 2 Gain.
4 One Event GOD.... Always Has, Many Reasons.
& How We Approach It....Effects Future Seasons.
Always Seek Peace....Heaping coals of Compassion.
Add A Dash Of Love....never to ration.
Welcome Good Evolution....bickering is for fools.
Under the influence of pride....lacking forgiving, tools.
Thru The Doorway Of Kindness....Heaven On Earth, Shall Be.
Thru The Clear Lens Of Love....hate can not see .
Always Welcome ....Peace As A Friend.
2 allow the fighting, 2 end !
A F I S H H H
History & Experience tell us that Moral Progress....
comes not in comfort & complacent times
but out of trial & confusion....Gerald Ford

ANGELS GATHERED.......

01-25-2014

The ANGELS gathered all around.
Without a word without a sound.
A WELCOMING PRESENCE filled the room.
As Another Soul began, 2 Bloom.
A whisper in the wind, Angel kissed.
As the ANGELS gathered in the Mist.
Faith 2 Believe 4 Second Sight.
As the Angels Led, 2 GOD'S LIGHT.
As the Angels Wings began 2 Spread.
The Image faded as the SPIRIT was LED.

MIRACLES IN ACTION.......BE OF PEACE.......05-01-2013

1st 2 last last 2 First, The Beginning End & BEGINNING......
REJOICE & LAUGH A LITTLE 2 !!!!!!!
LAST FLOETRY IN THIS SERIES.......
MIRACLES IN ACTION......4 NEEDED SATISFACTION
OF UNIVERSAL TRACTION....... YAY HAY HAY !

BE OF PEACE.......GOD IS ALIVE.......
BE OF PEACE.......LOVE SHALL SURVIVE.......
BE OF PEACE.......GOD SHALL GUIDE.......

BE OF PEACE.......HUMBLE THE RIDE.......
BE OF PEACE.......GOD KNOWS ALL.......
BE OF PEACE.......GOD GIVEN LAW.......
BE OF PEACE.......GOD SHALL BLESS.......
BE OF PEACE.......4 EQUAL SUCCESS.......
BE OF PEACE.......LOVE SHALL LEAD.......
BE OF PEACE.......gone the greed.......
BE OF PEACE.......PEACE SHALL BE.......
BE OF PEACE.......IN LIFES SEA.......
BE OF PEACE.......GOD SOW SAID.......
BE OF PEACE.......GOD'S NOT DEAD.......
BE OF PEACE.......HEAVEN ON EARTH.......
BE OF PEACE.......WORDS OF WORTH.......

4 FREEDOM.....

4 Freedom 2 exist, U must have LIBERTY.

Equal Rights, Education, Fruit 4 the individual Tree.

4 Freedom 2 exist, you must have Land 2 own.

4 All 2 Feed the Kin and Community, where seeds are sown.

4 Freedom 2 exist, the Spirit of the Lord must dwell.

4 that which is Glory, Guidance of the swell.

4 Freedom 2 thrive, U must feed and nourish it from within.

4 that which is Good, Will..... from here 2 there, beginning 2 end.

4 Freedom 2 exist U must have Silence, 2 Hear.

4 that which is GOD a Light of FAITH, Hope of Wit, 2 steer.

4 Freedom 2 exist, u can not be persuaded, by others.

Seek 2 study the past hate taught, and fed, in the sea of many brothers.

4 Freedom 2 Grow, U must be HUMBLE and Giving 2 the very Core.

2 not prey on the Meek, and Weak, or the Mother so poor.

4 Freedom 2 flourish, U must have a Education.

4 that which ends All poverty man made frustration.

4 Freedom 2 thrive the Spirit must be set Free.

without intimidation, or a catch 22, another frivols fee.

4 Freedom and Liberty, only GOD can give that 4 Sure.

And nations that eliminate, the predators, preying 4 more.

4 Freedom is a need, a GOD Given Right....a FOOD 4 All.

When GOD intervenes, its' from favoritism and pride 2 call.

4 Freedom has nothing 2 do with what you own or collect.

But whom who share with, and the Meek, U choose 2 Protect.

4 Freedom can not be bought, sold or traded, just Given.

BY GOD and feeding EQUAL Rights, granted in the sea of the Living.

4 Freedom is not others telling U what U can and can't do.

Freedom is a Blooming Miracle 4 All of the Loyal crew.

4 Freedom is Sparkle in the eyes, of a Family, lifted from poverty.

Where basic needs are met, Equal is the Blossom on Freedom's Tree.

4 Freedom is not a image a collection, or a swelling of pride.

4 Freedom is the Food Shared, 4 All not fed in the Universal Living Tide.

4 Freedom is shelter without the worry of being kicked out tomorrow.

4 Freedom is the Comfort in the storm, the tears of Joy and sorrow.

4 Freedom is of GOD without GOD Freedom can not exist.

4 GOD is the Guidance, the Purpose of Passion, in the Never ending mist.

4 Freedom is job security, business, Good 4 the Community.

As well as the Elders and the Young, far reaching, Love, Universally.

4 Freedom is the Food that feeds the SPIRIT of the Lord.

4 All of GOD CHOSEN....the Seal of the Guidance and Glory Sword.

4 Freedom is a Force where All are Treated Fair and with Grace.

Freedom is the FOOD of Life, thru all Time and Space.

4 Freedom is individual, and far reaching quite, Unique 4 All.

4 Freedom is the Liberty....2 Focus on a Solution, not the flaw.

4 Freedom is a GIFT from GOD, that can and has been taken away.

4 Freedom can exist not with favoritism and pride or ego in the way.

4 Freedom is EQUAL 4 every gender, income

as well as child tossed on the Street.

4 Freedom is the Food the staple, of providing 4 All Nourishment 2 eat.

4 Freedom is shelter, in the storm, when others tossed you out.

4 Freedom can exist not without Mercy 4 the Stranger or poor doubt.

4 Freedom does not boast or brag, or throw a distraction a full table snare.

4 Freedom is the Welcome mat, Thankful that the Guidance that is there.

4 Freedom is the TRUTH, not deceit, fed and bred 4 many a year.

4 Freedom is the Force of Knowing that GOD is Living, there is no fear..

4 Freedom is different 4 each, thru the journey of never ending Life.

The JOY of knowing the suffering was 2 Grow,

Learning from forced outside, strife.

4 Freedom is the Force from GOD, the reasons,

GOD, Humbled and parted the sea.

4 without Freedom and GOD there can exist

not the Fruit of Life and Liberty.

4 Freedom is a Treasure, of which 2 behold and admire.

4 without Freedom..... Liberty can not exist,

the Wings, of which 2 Fly Higher.

4 Freedom the definition, may be different 4 All, that's 4 Sure.

Yet Freedom must be fed....4 the SPIRIT of GOD, 2 Soar.

4 Freedom is a Gift a Priceless Treasure, that

can never be completely taken.

4 GOD is the SHIELD of LIBERTY.....4 a

Passion and Purpose, not 4-saken.

4 Freedom is the Food UNIVERSAL 4 All of mankind and Creatures.

4 Freedom is the Food of Life, that brings out the

SPIRIT of GOD the HOLY Features.

Many shall not think Freedom is that Important..... 4 All.

Thru the Valley of Life, nations that fed not Freedom GOD caused 2 fall.

4 the reasons were and are of pride, favoritism, oppression and suppression.

4 without FREEDOM 2 Grow....there can be no

UNIVERSAL, or inner National BLESISON. FREEDOM

Is The Nourishment Of KARING 4 ALL.

HONORING GOD'S COMMAND OF LOVE AS LAW !

THERES A SIDE 2 RAPE.......

05-16-2014.......

Theres a side 2 rape, thats not spoken.
Where Friendships are lost & Families are broken.
Theres a side 2 rape, that Touches Lives.
Where theres cultural silence, rape survives.
Theres a side of rape that blames for sure.
At times it's taught, their now unpure.
Theres a side 2 rape, when you just hear.
That can fill your thoughts with pain & fear.
Theres a side 2 rape, depending on whose involved.
If it's investigated or if it's solved.
Theres a side of rape if viewed by others.
More tend to become, lustul brothers.
Theres a side of rape, depending on whom.
If the Seed of Truth is Allowed To Bloom.
Theres a side of rape, even at war.
Thats not okay, thats' for Sure.
Theres a side of rape, all really should know.
When culturals deal with it, rape can't grow.
Theres a side of rape, many don't feel.
Most times were blamed, thats for real.
Theres a side 2 rape,when we can not provide.
In the wave of flashbacks, in Lifes tide.

Theres a side of rape, even with the eyes.

Theres lack of Respect, where Honor flies.

Theres a side of rape, depending on how many times.

How Wounded we become, from rape & crimes.

Theres a side of rape, that breaks the Bond of Trust.

Lots of times it's not talked about, uncontrolled lust.

Theres a side of rape, the guys gossip to.

And were are preyed on more, by a few.

Theres a side of rape, GOD Knows All.

And any type.... is against GOD'S Law !

Theres a side of rape, if its Us or a Friend.

That Wounds Our Soul, if Justice is pretend.

Theres a side of rape, if it's our Child.

In the Field of Life, where trust grows wild.

Theres a side of rape, when none care, if we tell.

Its alot more difficult, 4 us 2 get well.

Theres a side of rape, if we can't turn the page.

It effects Our Growth, in Lifes stage.

Theres a side of rape, that effects our trust.

Though it's not our fault, uncontrolled lust.

Theres a side of rape, if they have connections.

Our Friends will scatter, Our Past Protections

Theres a side of rape, that all should know.

If not dealt with Properly, the rapes will grow.

Theres a side of rape, that must be written & said.

When men seek to control their lust, rapes not fed.

Theres a side of rape, that can be a Good Thing 2.

Raise them Right, & the rapes will be few.

Theres a side of rape, Where We Can Relate To Others.

Mothers, Daughters, Friends.......Sisters, Brothers !

4 all those silent voices, really not heard.
Because in some societys, rapes a bad word.

The Doorway Of Freedom.... Opened On a Mid-Summers night.
Sent As Angels In The Mist,Of Loyalty's Light.
Thru The Doorway Of Action, 4 Kindness & Love Shared.
lest we never 4-get Those that Acted & Kared.
Without having to slight Her Children or forced, to be unknown.
Honoring The Gift Of Life ....Where Love & Loyality is Grown.
Thru the Doorway Of Inspiration & Empowerments Effect !
Undercover Angels Sent....2 Welcome & Protect .
She Felt Their Presence In Town, That Day.
Thank GOD 4 All, Who Welcome Per Say.
They Called Themselves.... The Band Of Brothers.
That Treat With Respect, All Sisters & Mothers.
Thru the Doorway Of Freedom, they were bullied, no more.
On The Wings Of Liberty, Their Lives Did Soar !

ATTITUDE GRATITUDE....

06-9-2014

Every obstacle is a Challenge....With A Thankful Attitude.
Much Can be Accomplished....With Humble Gratitude.
One Of Growth & Clarity....Thru Peaceful Evolution.
4 Contentment Of All....& Honorable Resolution.
Thru The Doorway Of 4-Giveness....Peace Can Really be.
Add A Dash Of Compassion....& Humble Humility.
GOD Gives Us Challenges....2 See If We blame.
Or View it As A Blesison....4 Betterment, 2 Gain.
4 One Event GOD.... Always Has, Many Reasons.
& How We Approach It....Effects Future Seasons.
Always Seek Peace....Heaping coals of Compassion.
Add A Dash Of Love....never to ration.
Welcome Good Evolution....bickering is for fools.
Under the influence of pride....lacking forgiving, tools.
Thru The Doorway Of Kindness....Heaven On Earth, Shall Be.
Thru The Clear Lens Of Love....hate can not see .
Always Welcome ....Peace As A Friend.
2 allow all the fighting, 2 end !

If you see me on the Street, just Look 4 the a Smile, on my face.
4 I am One of many a Mixture of many, types, of blood and many a race.
I was Born of GOD and I would not be here if wasn't 4 the Gift of Life.

4 being many makes Life, Cool, without the burdens of comparing strife.

4 the American Blend, U need not be One

color One gender, or One Religion.

4 the Freedom 2 Chose, is Liberty, a, personal decision..

You will see many types of cultures All mixed into One, 4 Sure.

ONE Blood One GOD, One peoples, now that's a Universal cure.

You may not agree at all, yet if you Look thru

the lens of Humble Humility.

The beating Heart is what matters, not the outside you see, Visually.

If I could choose 2 be just One, I would not even go that path at All.

4 the GOD I know ....is Universal, and Loving, now that a Humble call.

ALL IS POSSIBLE.......

01-10-2014

ALL IS POSSIBLE WITH GOD'S GRACE.
ALL IS POSSIBLE, THRU TIME & SPACE.
ALL IS POSSIBLE YES INDEED.
ALL IS POSSIBLE WITH GOD SEED.
ALL IS POSSIBLE, HUMOUR 2.
ALL IS POSSIBLE 4 GOD'S CREW.
ALL IS POSSIBLE CHALLENGES GALORE.
ALL IS POSSIBLE THRU GOD'S DOOR.
ALL IS POSSIBLE IN GOD'S TIDE.
ALL IS POSSIBLE HUMBLE THE RIDE !!!!!!!

A NEIGHBOR IN NEED......

There once was a Neighbor, a Neighbor In Need.
The Son stepped 4th 4 Faith w/ Actions Feed.
The Mom said no way, you can't go.
Mom He Spoke what of Neighborly Reap Sow?
The Son Spoke, Mom you Tithe and Attend.
Yet a Neighbor In Need, you will not defend.
A Miracle In Action I Witnessed that Day.
When One Stepped 4th Faith With Actions way.
A Kind & Courtous Attitude 4 Sure.
Good Intentions, and Good Works, Oh Sow Pure.
With A Smile We drove off, on A Mission of Kare.
I Thank GOD Everyday 4 a Son willing 2 Share.
In a Time Of Need, Actions Of Loving Grace.
And That in itself, Makes the World a Better Place.

4 Balbao Hay House....

IN GOD'S LIGHT....

In God's Light,
There Is Sight.

In God's Reign,
There Is Gain.

In God's Care,
There Is Fair.

In God's Instruction,
There Is Production.

In God's Grace,
There's Every Race.

In God's Season,
There Is Reason.

In God's Living,
There Is Giving.

In God's Root,
There Is Fruit.

In God's Story,
There Is Glory.

In God's Conception,
There Is Protection.

In God's Birth,
There Is Worth.

In God's Trinity,
There Is Infinity.

In God's Gleeming,
There Is Meaning.

In God's Evolution,
There Is Resolution.

In God's Inspiration.
There Is Jubilation!

Thru God's Door.
Love So Pure !

IN GOD'S HANDS.......

In GOD'S HANDS, there is JOY LOVE and INSPIRATION.
In GOD'S HANDS, There is COMFORT,
WISDOM and JUBILATION.
In GOD'S LIGHT, there is GLORY in FAITH and ETERNITY.
In GOD"S LIGHT, there A LOVING SHIELD,
A PROMISE, of EQUALTY.
In GOD'S GLORY, there is LAW, EQUAL LAW, 4 ALL.
In GOD'S GLORY, there is GUIDANCE A ROCK a WALL.
In GOD'S LOVE, there is a ANCIENT SUPERNATURAL POWER.
In GOD"S LOVE, there is a Uniqness, where all a budding FLOWER.
In GOD'S COMFORT, there are LOVING Ears
that hear every Heartfelt PRAYER.
In GOD'S COMFORT, there is a Belief in Every, JOYFUL, Layer.
In GOD"S KNOWLEDGE< there is DIVINE
WISDOM, no amount of money can buy.
In GOD"S KNOWLEDGE, there is
INSTRUCTION, 4 the Impossible, 2 FLY.
In GOD"S MERCY, there is a LOVE< that
WORDS can not EXPRESS.
In GOD"S MERCY, there is a POWER, of JOY 2 BLESS.
In GOD'S SHELTER, there is a Kindness,
4 HOPE 4 ALL 2 SUCCEED.
In GOD"S SHELTER, there is a Appreciation 4 the tinest of SEED.

In GOD"S SEA OF ETERNAL LIFE HOPE is the
NOURISHMENT, that Leads & Feeds.
In GOD"S Sea OF ETERNAL LIFE, there are
a INFINITE No of Glorious SEEDS.
In GOD"S POMISE 2 the FAITHFUL, there shall be
PEACE ON EARTH & LOVE is the SOLUTION.
In GOD"S PROMISE Of ETERNAL GRACE,
GOOD WILL 4 ALL IS EVOLUTION.
IN GOD"S PEACE, there resides the KEY 2 ETERNITY.
That resides within the FAITH, of U and Me.
IN GOD"S HOLY LIGHT, THERE IS LOVE
4 ETERNITY, 2 BELIEVE.
IN SOWING THE SEEDS OF KINDNESS
4 MIRACLES 2 ACHIEVE.......

IN OTHERS....

When We Invest In Others Futures & are not just seeking to aquire.

We Can Be A Part Of Opportuinities, That Create & Inspire.

One Key 2 Elevation Is Good-Will & Encouragment to Others.

4 The Empowerement Of those suppressed, Sisters & Brothers.

One Person at A Time not just millions to the unknown.

2 Witness The Effects, Of Loving Fruits, that Are Grown.

A Key To Feeling Welcomed, is the opposite of neglect.

4 the Nourishment Of Love, With Good Givings Effect.

Not 2 be rich or famous but 4 All Upon Earth.

4 Missions Of Purpose & PosItive Worth !

4 Miracles In Action, 4 the World a Better Place.

2 Empower One & All Thru Out All Time & Space.

4 its not what we aquire, but the legacy we leave behind.

Whether we chose to be selfish or Considerate & Kind.

4 The Spirit Of Giving.... Is Most Powerful Indeed.

By Nourishing Good-Will.... not gluttony of greed !

IN SPIRIT....

That Cheerfully Shared, Be It Wisdom Or Grace.
Continues On, Thru-Out All Time & Space.
Walking In GOD' S Truth, Is Fine Indeed.
4 Its All About Love, not ego or greed.
Entertain The Stranger The Poor & All.
4 Love In Action A Jolly Good Call.
Thirst 4 Humour Share A Good Laugh.
4 A Positive Purpose In Lifes Living Path.
4 Tis Better 2 Be Poor Homeless & Broke.
Yet Rich In Spirit & Share A Good Joke.
Its All About Actions Not Words Many Throw.
& Seeking 2 Empower.... 4 Freedom 2 Flow !
Guard The gossip always, 4 Life Never Ends.
Welcome One & All.... 4 Eternal Loyal Friends.
Seek 2 Give Glory 2 GOD & Do A Good Deed.
Be At Peace In Knowing, Love Is A Endless Feed.
It's not what you own that says who you are.
But The Imprint In The Wake, A Smile Or A scar ?
4 All Those You Meet, 4 You Really Never Know.
If They Are Angels In Desquise, Sent 4 Wisdom 2 Grow !

IN THE DEPTHS OF A TEARDROP....

In the Depths Of A Teardrops Gentle Flow.

One Can Experience....Letting Go.

In the Depths Of A Teardrops, Lingering Laugh.

One Can Experience ....A Humourous Path.

In the Depths Of A Teardrop Flowing Free.

One Can Experience, A Purity.

In The Depths Of A Teardrops Gentle Fall.

Theres Enough Power, 2 Break Down A wall.

In The Depths Of A Teardrops Emotional Ride.

Be Thankful 4.... The Tears You've Cried.

Be It From Joy or Sorrow, Let Them Flow.

4 The Inner You...2 Really Grow !

INSTRUMENTS OF LAW.......

02/01/2014

INSTRUMENTS OF LAW...TOOLS 4 THE LIVING.
PRAISE BE 2 GOD...GRACE 4 THE GIVING.
INSTRUCTION INDEED...AMAZING EVOLUTIONS.
4 ON EARTH GLORY... GODLY SOLUTIONS !
GODLY SEEDS...4 DIVINE SATISFACTION.
4 ON EARTH GLEE ...TRUTHFULL TRACTION.
ANGELS IN THE MIST...ANGELS IN DESQUISE.
IN THE SEA OF LIFE...WHERE TRUE FAITH FLYS !

Let All....

Let All Who Have Ears, Let them hear.
GOD Commands PEACE, Oh Sow Clear.
Let All Who Eyes Let Them See.
GOD Commands LOVE, 4 Humanity.
Let All Who have A Concious, Really Know.
GOD Commands HONOR, Of All Reap Sow.
Let those who promote pride, vengence & war.
Be Led BY LOVE, 4 A Purpose So Pure.
Let All who bicker battle & fight.
Know GOD IS Love, & Love Is Light.
Let All Seek Peace & Humbleness 2.

So hate isn't fed, & Love Get's Thru !

Jesus Returned....4 GOD'S GLORY....

Jesus Returned In The Form Of Another.
Thru The Valley Of Time, As A Poor Mother.
2 Witness The Treatment Of Women On Earth.
4 The Glory Of Teaching, Merciful Morals Of Worth.
As A Female He Was exploited. oppressed, treated as less.
In Many nations lusted after w/o Respect 2 Address.
There was lack Of Appreciation 4 The Womb Of Life.
Being not Welcomed only added 2 poverty & strife.
Some were totally abandoned w/o a safe place to live.
Even though many had the Resources to Cheerfully Give.
Some were forced into exile, & their Children 2.
From pride in males, not allowing Peace 2 Get Thru.
His next Journey was a Prisoner falsley convicted.
While He was doing time, His Family was evicted.
Some Nations made their funds by judging others.
Without GOD'S Approval, 4 suppression only smothers.
The real perp got off having the funds to pay.
Allowing injustice & corruption, from greed in the way.
He Witnessed How some Gov didn't Empower but oppress.
Not Welcoming Freedom & Liberty 4 Equalty & Success.
How some made millions while others were tossed out.
Without A Place 2 Call Home on lifes Living route.
There were many places, yet Families could not Live.
From Nations not Seeking 2 Welcome Serve & Give.
Jesus Returned 2 The Creator, with a list quite long.
Of wars favortism & corruption lacking LOVE Sow Strong.

So GOD Sent The ARK Angels, In The Form Of The Living.

2 Teach Gratitude & Glory, The Joy Of Cheerfull Giving.

Thru The Doorway Of Faith Peace Love & Grace.

A World once lost, became a Better Place !

As Peoples Learned Peacemaking 4 Purposes Of Positive Worth.

Love Was Spread & Fed.... 4 Kindness Upon Earth.

GOD Even Gave LAW, 4 All, Easy 2 Understand.

2 Nourish Equalty & Allow Freedom 2 Stand.

man made law disappeared, in the wave of Lifes tide.

As Humbleness Was Welcomed, gone was the pride.

Equal Justice & Harmony, 4 Merciful Instruction.

Brought 4th Fruit Of Love, 4 Positive Production!

Reap Sowing Of Peace & Empowerment, 4 Funds On Earth.

Matters Indeed, 4 Proper Merciful Morals, Of Worth.

2 reap sow of exploitation and corruption is a no no.

2 Reap Sow Of Honor Is A Nutrient 4 LOVE 2 Grow.

Doing Unto Others As U Would Have Done 2 U.

Honoring That One Law, Allowed Love 2 Get Thru.

Jesus didn't return 2 condem but Teach The Living.

The Euphoric Joy Of Love When Souls Are Giving.

4 hate can not be spread when Love is applied.

4 2 Serve GOD Is 2 Welcome Humbleness, In Lifes Tide.

2 Give Thanks 2 GOD, & Cheerfully step back.

4 Others 2 Feel Welcomed, 4 Love 2 not lack.

2 Really Serve the Living GOD Of All Creation.

Is 2 Welcome Kindness, not war & exploitation.

Nourishing Peace & Prosperity Equal Rights 4 All.

2 Welcome & Honor GOD'S Command Of Love, As Law

Enter at your own risk, the sign said above.

No hitting or pushing, try not to shove.

Please Be Silent, lay your Heart, on this plate.

Something you'd like to say, before it's too late?

Please... no excuses or lies, for I will know.

I expect the Truth, 4 Honesty...2 grow

I'll ask the questions, you please, respond.

The truth... is a requirement, I know, when I'm conned

Remember back in 83, when you hurt, that child?

Forever the Spirit was gone, meek and mild.

remember the friend whom just wanted the Truth.

4 ommission was the order, a destructive, slueth.

You must pay a price, for these, blows to the mind.

You walked around heartless, Compassion blind.

Whom did U Love, unconditionally, what did u say.

U boarded the boat, of let's trash them 2-day.

I see U loved your spouse, but your kids were tossed.

Do U not understand, that;'s a line that shouldn't, be crossed.

Not 2 enable or baby, but allow them 2 prosper and fly away.

u actually hindered the growth, with greed in the way.

What about the trashing of another's name, when they weren't around.

Did U not know GOD is aware of every action, every sound?

What about the lies U constantly tried 2 cover up and hide.

Did U not know that's a symptom of ignorance and pride.

What about the way, you spoke to your grandmom and grandad?

Thru the angry glass, you couldn't see, they were sad.

My... you look shocked son, we've just begun.

I am going back, until the good deed, work... is done.

Please don't interrupt, wipe the tears, from your face.

The Book of Life is open, we've run out, of space.

I tried to help you, avoid this, destructive mess.
You refused my signs, didn't repent or confess.
I sent many angels, without wings, your way.
Not once... did you care, what, they had... to say.
I gave you many chances, son, now... accept, fate.
4... you must go back, Eternal wings.... will have to wait.

Is is possible 4 One 2 relay or relate, 2 that which they did not see?

As my mind drifts, back 2 a Poem written by Francis Scott Key.

Without the Living experience, could One have felt such, devotion?

4 that which was written, from observing, the

FLAG, raised, from the ocean.

Is it possible 2 actually feel or experience, that which is a part of History?

Can you really put the Glory it into Words,

without walking in the shoes of thee?

The emotion One can feel, with simple words

that touch the Soul and Heart.

Could One of really written such a Warming Poem

without Living, experience, the part?

As the emotions run wild, just Imagine thru

the eyes, of One who was there.

waiting Patiently 2 see, if anything was left,

standing in the wake of war's snare.

As the bomb's burst, 4 many days, drifting in the sea, without a clue.

Of what would be left in the wake, of war,

once the deafening noise was thru.

As I ponder these thoughts, and the emotions

released, in just Simple Words written.

I have come 2 understand that experience must

occur, 4 the Passion 2 be smitten.

Just a simple Flag, of large size, hand made with

much Love, Honor and Appreciation.

That played a very Important role in the Future

History, of Loyalty, Humility, and dedication.

What must it of felt like, 2 believe that another

nation, was in over their head.

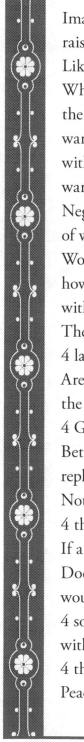

Imagine the feeling of relief, when the Flag was
raised, and thousands weren't dead.
Like a beacon in the sky, that could be seen, 4 many miles.
What must it have been like 2 feel the Glory of
the Flag, seen thru the LIVING Trials.
war not spoke of much, some believe it's all about an eye 4 an eye.
without a clue of wits, compassion, at times secrets of which, 2 get by.
war, usually a battle over land which others, believe it's okay 2 impose.
Neglecting the fact of Life, that it raises the Fruit
of which, where Freedom grows.
Would it be worth it 2 battle over, a 25 mile stretch of Land.
how many innocent Lives should be taken, as pride makes it's stand.
with war brings poverty suffering, when nations are willing 2 let go.
Then Unity is acquired a Tool needed 4 All of which 2 thrive and grow.
4 land that is Given in PEACE, 2 share amongst the many nations.
Are a Fruit a Ark a Act of Humility, 4 Unity in
the sea of many Trials and Revelations.
4 GOD spoke of that which is GOOD 4 All, in more than One way.
Better 2 Give than receive, and GOD shall
replace with better, what U gave away.
Not in being weak, or a wimp, so that poverty doesn't grow more.
4 there are many unseen rippling consequences from the act of war.
If a nation works with others, example speaking 2 the enemy.
Does that not make them Wiser, 4 only a fool,
would try not 2 make Peace with thee.
4 some there shall never be satisfaction, bullies
with the want 2 have and control it all.
4 thru out All nations History's, tis better 2 make
Peace, then cause more 2 needlessly, fall.

As I ponder theses thoughts of a Flag raised, in the
Historical sea of many needless, storms.
I have come 2 the conclusion there are times when man's senses, are thorns.

A short Poem written on scrap paper, yet 4-Ever, 2 change a nation 4 sure.
2 day seek 2 Imagine the relief, of a sign, with
nothing said, seen from the shore.
A battle of many bombs, 4 days and days on end.
Imagine the Glorious sight of the Flag, still blowing in the wind.
4 it is not spoke of much, Living History, felt
and Experienced, relayed and written.
yet at Times it Touches another personally, with
Love and Emotions, quite smitten.
Imagine had he not had a Friend whom had the means 2 publish and share.
Would the Gift of this Experienced Emotion, been
felt, or hidden from poverty's snare ?
Can One actually write a Poem of Grace and
Glory that Touches the Heart so.
Not without the Living experience, 2 Freely share with others....2 Grow !

SEEK OF....

Seek not wealth, nor lots of riches.
Seek 2 Sow, Giving Stitches.
Seek not vengence nor vanity.
Seek 2 Sow, Humble Hospitality.
Seek not ego nor pride.
Seek 2 Welcome A Humble Side.
Seek not ignorance nor deception.
Seek All Truth....4 Protection.
Seek nor bittereness nor war.
Seek All Peace, thats 4 Sure.
Seek not favortism nor exclusion.
Seek 2 Welcome 4 Inclusion.
Seek not 2 reap/sow of corruption.
Seek Honor Of Funds, 4 Production.
Seek not 2 separate nor divide.
Seek Unity In Lifes Tide.
Seek not violence nor intimadation.
Seek Peace As A Proclaimation.
Seek not secrets 2 evolve.
Seek Honesty 2 Resolve.
Seek not doubt, nor lust.
Seek Faith & Hope 2 Trust.
Seek not materilsm of worldy worth.
Seek Of Love, 4 Peace On Earth !

SMILING SANTA 4 YOUTH.....& ALL !!!!!

Smiling Santa Arrived 4 Your List Of Good Deeds.
How You Assisted Others With Basic Needs
Be It Doing The Dishes Or Helping With Chores.
Or Picking Up Litter Or Opening Doors.
Never Pick Up The Trash On The Road.
Thats For The Adults & Kindness Showed.
Did You Report a bully, Let Someone Know ?
Or Sit With Grandma Learning How To Sew ?
Were You Nice On The Bus Offer A Seat ?
Or Assist With The Drinks & Food To Eat ?
Do You Have Any Animals That Need Care ?
What About The Fish, They Know Your There.
Did You Be Good In The Car For A Ride ?
It's Good To Be Kind & not full of pride.
Did You Relay A Message Or Assist A Friend ?
Did You Tell The Truth For Honor To Defend ?
Did You Pick Up After Yourself Clean Your Room ?
Plant A Tree Or Flower & Wait For It To Bloom ?

Did You Give A Ride To Another You Know Thats Poor?

Make Sure You Ask A Adult First Thats For Sure.

Were You Kind To Your Teacher Sister Or Brother?

Did You Speak Nicely To All, Including Your Mother ?

Did You Throw A Fit Or Be Mean At The Store ?

Seek To Always Be Thankful & Nice Thats For Sure.

Did You Be Kind To The Student, Others Exclude ?

Always Be Nice, Know Matter Your Mood.

Did You Share A Book & Not Watch Too Much T.V ?

Did You Tell A Funny Joke, For Kindness Is Free ?

Did You Help Your Brother or Throw A Fit ?

Did You Listen To A Elder, If They Ask You To Sit ?

Did You Put On Your Seatbelt If There Is One ?

Did You Take The Time To Have A Little Fun?

Did You Be Nice To Others & Learn How To Share?

Thats Kindness In Action ....Showing You Care.

Did You Remember Your Prayers & Wish Good For All.

Did You Remember To Relay A Message Even A Call.

Always Make Sure It's Okay To Answer The Phone.

Get Your Parents Permission, Even When Alone.

Did You Pick On Any Due To Where They Live?

Thats Not Nice Seek Always Kind Words To Give.

Did You Tease Because Of Their Car Or How They Dress.

Thats Not A Good Deed Either Seek Kind Words To Adress.

Did You Look Both Ways Before You Crossed The Street.

Did You Remember To Brush Your Teeth & Wash Your Feet?

Did You Tell If Someones Mean Even With Speech ?

Did You Sit Still & Be Quiet While One Was Trying To Teach?

Did You Seek To Be Kind To All Even The Sick?

Don't Eat Or Drink After Them, Even A Lick.

Did You Say No To Any That Tried To Get You To Drink ?
Alcohol Or Drugs It Will Effect How You Act & Think.

Did You Be Nice To The Busdriver & To All.
Thats Important Love Is A Good Law.
If Your Friend Is Being Bullied Tell Another.
That Matters To, Maybe Your Big Brother.
Make Sure To Tell A Adult You Know & Trust.
Being Honest About This, Is Always A Must.
Did You Offer To Asist When You Knew It Was A Need ?
They Shouldn't Have To Ask, Kindness Is A Good Deed !
Did You Tell Your Parents, If Someone Was Mean In School.
Even If Its A Teacher Or Janitor, Kindness Is A Rule .
Did You Tell The Truth About A Gun, Even If It Was Hidden?
Always Ask Or Tell A Adult & Touching It's Forbidden.
If Your Parents Are There & It's For Food.
Remember Always Its Not Nice To Be Rude.
Never Point It At Another Don't Pick It Up Or Touch.
For Many People Love You Very Very Much !

Did You Remember To Say Thank You, When Any Are Nice.
Thats A Good Deed To, Called Action Of Word Sacrifice.
Did You Be Kind On The Bus Or In The Car All Around.
Thats Important Some Are Very Effected By Sound.
Do You Believe In Angels & Lots Of Love ?
For GOD Is On Earth As In The Heavens Above.
Share Your List For Santa & Include Your Good Deeds.
Maybe Santa Will Bring You A Pack Of Flower Seeds .
For Love Is Within Kindness & In Doing Good Things.
Most Of All Don't Forget To Laugh....

TEARS OF JOY IT BRINGS !

& Remember It's Okay To Cry....
Be It For Joy Or Sorrow.
For Things Will Get Better....
For Theres Always Tomorrow !
Alsow Remember To Cheerfully Share, Wisdom
& Knowledge ....You Learned.
For That Matters Most Of All, Not How
Much Money....You Have Earned !
SHARE A LAUGH.... IN LIFES PATH !

STAND YOUR GROUND....

08-20-2014

Stand Your Ground.... but Welcome One.
Seek 4-Giveness & Grace 4 Fun.
Stand Your Ground....In Good Cheer.
Be Of Love not hate or fear.
Stand Your Ground....w/o suppression.
4 Freedom 2 Endure, As A Lesson !
Stand Your Ground....4 Whats Right.
But Always Keep Peace, Peace In Sight.
Stand Your Ground....With Evolution.
Know Good Change Creates Solution.
Stand Your Ground....With Education.
w/o violence or threats of intimadation.
Stand Your Ground....4 Everyones Child.
So They Know Peace, Where Love Is Filed.
Stand Your Ground....& Save A Life.
4 Peace On Earth, not war & strife.
Stand Your Ground.... with Good Will.
Learn Proper Peacemaking, As a Skill.
Stand Your Ground ....In A Loving Way.
Know it matters what You do & say.
Stand Your Ground... with out destruction.
Be Merciful & Kind, 4 Peaceful Production !

Stand Your Ground...w/o murder or hate.

Heaping Coals Of Compassion, On Lifes Plate.

Stand Your Ground... 4 Gratitude & Respect.

So Many Can Enjoy, True Beauty's Effect.

Stand Your Ground.... & Share It 2.

4 It Belongs 2 GOD.... not just You!

Stand Your Ground....But Most Of All.

Honor GOD'S Command, Of Love As Law !

THE POWER OF TRUTH SHALL REIGN & RULE.

THE POWER OF TRUTH, 4 OF GOD TOOL.

THE POWER OF TRUTH, 4 GODLY LAW.

THE POWER OF TRUTH, 4 ONE & ALL.

THE POWER OF TRUTH w/o confusing stipulations.

THE POWER OF TRUTH, 4 LOVE & INSPIRATIONS.

THE POWER OF TRUTH, 4 GODLY REAP SOW.

THE POWER OF TRUTH, 4 ALL 2 KNOW.

THE POWER OF TRUTH, UNIVERSAL GOD'S TIDE.

THE POWER OF TRUTH, gone the pride.

THE POWER OF TRUTH, 4 HEAVEN ON EARTH.

THE POWER OF TRUTH, 4 LAWS OF WORTH !!!!!!!!!

IN GOD'S TRUTH THERE IS LIGHT.

IN GOD'S LOVE THERE IS SIGHT !

The Presence Of Truth....

The Presence Of Truth, Shall be Known.

Within The Seeds That Are Sown.

Nourishment Of Euphoric Love.

4 Peace On Earth As Above.
Good News & Glory Of Godly Light.
4 Love In Action Faith In Flight.
4 Joy Hope & Inspiration.
4 Peace In Action & Jubilation.
doubt not fret not 4 GOD'S Shield.
Welcome Peace & Seek 2 Yield.
Allow GOD 2 Guide 4 Equal Law.
4 Love 2 Lead & Peace 4 All !

THE SEEDS WE SOW....

02/07/2014

THE SEEDS WE SOW...HELP US GROW.
THE LOVE WE SHARE...HELP US KARE.
THE DEEDS WE GIVE...HELP US LIVE.
THE FRUITS WE NOURISH...HELP US FLOURISH.
THE CHALLENGES WE ACHIEVE...HELP US BELIEVE.
4 THE SEEDS SOWN, ARE NOT OUR OWN.
4 IT'S WHAT WE GIVE, THAT HELP US LIVE !

Theres a side of Education....

Theres a side of Education, many don't Know.
Where Creative Thinking is lost & suppression does flow.
Theres a side of Education, that stops progress in action.
Where Uniqueness isn't Welcomed w/o True satisfaction.
Theres a side of Education thats a True Blesison Indeed.
Where its not about priviledge prosperity & greed.
Theres a side of Education, One Must Experience 2 Know.
4 Knowledge 2 be Nourished & Wisdom 2 Really Flow.
Theres a side of Education where Individuality is out.
Where Thinkers are suppressed from rules no doubt.
There is a side of Education that can Give Rebirth 2 a Nation.
And Empower & Enlighten, Every Generation.

Theres a side of Education Where Voices aren't heard.

From rules for fools, lack of Proper Word.

Theres a side of Education that oppresses Learning.

Where its not about Giving Back but what you are earning.

Theres a side of Education where it adds lots of stress.

Full of fees and rules lacking Freedom To Address.

Theres a side of Education where crimes aren't reported.

Where greed comes first & Truth isn't Supported.

Thers a side of Education where theres to many deadlines to meet.

Where Families must chose between Seeking & Food 2 Eat.

Theres a side of Education where upward Action is lost.

When its not about Uniqueness but how much it cost.

Theres a side of Education where there are to many rules.

When bullies are created from lack of Proper Teaching Tools.

Theres a side of Education where the staff is excluded.

Where the Cooks & Janitors Ideas aren't

Welcomed from priviledge polluted.

Theres a side of Education where many voices aren't heard.

From to many in a classroom overwhelmed & absurd.

Theres a side of Education that can bring much Joy 2 Life.

That can touch many lives & ease lots of strife.

Theres a side of Education that really does Protect.

When All Feel Welcomed & Are Treated with Respect.

Theres a side of Education full of deadlines & fees.

Where the True Joy Of Learning is lost in the breeze.

Theres a side of Education, where all can Love 2 Learn.

Where Uniqueness Is Welcomed & Seeking 2 Yearn.

Theres a side of Education, when its not all about dough.

That can Nourish Whole Nations, 2 Thrive & Grow.

Theres a side of Education w/o suppression man made pollution.

That can Empower & Enlighten 4 Good Evolution.

Theres a side of Education that can Open Many A Door.

Where All Are Inspired 2 Experience & Explore.

Theres a side of Education that can Light The flame of Seeking.

Viewing Thru The Lens Of A Microscope without any Speaking.

Theres a side Of Education that can be Good Evolution.

Without to many rules or wealth priviledge pollution.

Theres a side of Education that Cna Be The Very Best.

4 A Life Of Neverending Learning 4 Seekings Quest.

Theres a side of Education when Nourished at any age.

That can Open many a Doors In Lifes Living Page.

Theres a side of Education that can Touch The Body As A Whole.

While Caressing The Mind & Spirit While Nourishing The Soul.

Theres a side Of Education, 4 All 2 Really Seek & Explore.

Where Ideas Are Welcomed & Creativety Does Soar.

Theres a side of Education, Thats a True Blesison Indeed.

Where It All About Empowerment, not suppression & greed.

Theres a side Of Education Where Freedom Does Flow.

Where All Are Welcomed ....4 Knowledge to Grow !

AN ANGEL...

I saw an Angel, with eyes of blue.

I saw an Angel, higher she flew.

I saw an Angel, with a smile, so bright.

I saw an Angel, with her wings, she took flight.

I saw an Angel...in the skies above.

I saw an Angel...filled with love.

I saw an Angel, following another.

I saw an Angel..like no other.

I saw an Angel, with eyes of grey.

I saw an Angel, gently, fly away.

I saw an Angel, save a child.

I saw an Angel, where Faith grows wild.

I saw an Angel...in the eyes of a dove.

I saw an Angel...spreading Peace and Love.

I saw an Angel...in the depths of a good deed.

I saw an Angel, gentle was the seed.

I saw an Angel...in the hands of my dad.

I saw an Angel...4 that I am glad.

I saw an Angel...with no words spoken.

I saw an Angel...Heavens token.

I saw an Angel, heard the wings.

I saw an Angel, where harmony sings.

I saw an Angel, gentle was she.

I saw an Angel...light and free.

I saw an Angel...Mary was her name.
I saw an Angel... light Hopes flame.
I saw an Angel...felt the dew.
I saw an Angel...with wings she flew.
I saw an Angel...gentle and free.
I saw an Angel...in Hopes sea.
I saw an Angel..like no other.
I saw an Angel..in the heart of my mother.
I saw an Angel...in the sea of change.
I saw an Angel...in lifes range.
I saw an Angel, gentle was he.
I saw an Angel light and free.
I saw an Angel...a friend in season.
I saw an Angel...friendship's reason.
I saw an Angel...thru the heart of another.
I saw an Angel...Within, my brother.
I saw an Angel...in the sky.
I saw an Angel, take flight and fly.
I saw an Angel, that I know.
I saw an Angel...from, HEAVENS glow.

FRIENDSHIP FARE...

A friend... is a flicker, a light in the...deep dark.
A twinkle in the eye, when love, is the spark.
A friend... puts friendship, before that, destructive mate.
A healing tool...where personal growth... is the fate.
A friend cherishes the tears, you've both cried.
A wake of learning...in the friendship... tide
A friend... is content, 2 love you, just the way, you are.
Through the good times and bad, a friendship... scar.
A friend... does good deeds, you know, just because.
They know... your unique, including the flaws.
A friend... is the calm, in the middle of a wake.
Advice is real... personal growth... isn't fake.
A friend... is still loyal, even when, your not, there.
With, good things, 2 say... friendship fare.
A friend... is the comfort, in the midst, of a storm.
Hugs are real, and the heart beats... warm.
A friend... is a treasure, not of silver and gold.
But of laughter and cheer, as the memories, unfold.
A friend speaks the Truth without omission.
Knowing it matters, Honesty of a Mission
A friend... is unique, rare, is the breed.
Caressing the soul, with a... Compassionate seed.

2 all those friends who stuck, around.
And those who have yet...2 B found

FEATHER...

Light and free, fragile as a feather.
Used 4 centuries, as an emotional tether.
Comfort and warmth, 2 surround the soul.
Ancient Voices...Wisdom of gold.
The air that you breathe, fire in the sky.
A tool used... that help, many get by.
The sound of Joy, a heart full of Peace.
Spreading like wildfire, a spiritual release.
The mountain so high, the rippling of water.
2 help you get by, when you falter.
A priceless diamond... a ruby so red.
Used 4 the mind, 2 keep you, fed.
A tower of glass, with windows of gold.
2 keep you protected, from the cold.
A feeling of euphoria, like know other.
When you, take my hand,as a spiritual brother.
A light in the dark, 2 help lead the way.
2 reach my floor, you must take the time, 2 Pray.
A force 2 be reckoned with...Angels in flight.
Just reach 4 me...2 tuck you, in at night.
A gentle hand, 2 keep you afloat.
4 i am ...The Spiritual Boat.

HARRIET...

I knew what I wanted 2 be...after I read the Book.

Just 2 be sure...I gave it,another look.

Amazed I was at a tender, young age.

Excited 2 turn, another page.

When times, were difficult, I would drift back.

2 an Amazing Lady...who cut no slack.

Fearless and brave...although, not full of pride.

This lady, continued on...many had 2 hide.

From man and his force, against hate and oppression.

After reading this book, I gained a Timeless... lesson.

That ONE person...could Help change the World, if they gave it, there all.

4 this journey, reminded me, of another,under Compassion's, Humble call.

4 JESUS...Full of Love...a Merciful Giver, was he & she.

That lead the way...4 individuals, like you, and me.

When I finished the Book of Harriet Tubbman, and her quiet, force.

4 -ever my life was changed..., from readings powerful, course.

I read the Book again, and I knew, what I wanted, 2 be.

A PEACEMAKER...4 Equality...in Life's social, cup of tea.

a small little lady...with Amazing, Courage, Hope and Grace..

who made a difference, 4 many... in History's, true trace.

Not 2 be famous, or rich... but just because.

She saw the heart...without the judge mental, flaws.

many passed thru the underground, Railroad...

with Hope, and Freedom, in Sight.

Because one little lady...cared 2 take action....4 what's morally, right..

So...What I want 2 Be...when I grow up, is Humble and meek.

2 care enough 2 take action...instead of turn, the other cheek.

not 4 hate or bitterness, but 4 the Peaceful, Equal call.

2 Love unconditionally, including the flaw.

2 see not the race, religion, disability, gender or color.

but 2 Love One another... as a sister, or brother.

PRIORITY 4 SOCIETY.....

My job is Vital 2 thy nation, although I am not paid.

My career is for a Lifetime, for Honor of Moral Grade.

Most Times my finances are quite bleak, with bills I can't pay.

Although I THANK GOD 4 the Gift of a Child, each and everyday.

I am the Doctor, the Counsler the carpooler, each day is quite Unique.

I am the Listener the Teacher, the mediator in the Responsibilty creek.

I am the opps missed the Bus-Driver, the shoefinder, drying teenage tears.

It's a Lifetime commitment, thru out the many stages and rages and years.

There was time when One could stay Home,

and raise the Children with ease.

Now it's quite difficult 2 make ends meet, with so many bills in the breeze.

Some will argue non-stop without a clue of

trying 2 make it on mininum wage.

When it comes 2 suffering and sacrifice they

have yet 2 turn that Living page.

My motto is if I work full time whom is raising

the Child, whom is Looking out.

Just try comparing childcare fees, where The Importance

of raising youth is a priority, no doubt.

There are vacations that never occured and places we have never seen.

Although I would not trade any of it 4 want of the financial green.

I have witnessed the latchkey syndrome where nobodys Home.

And the children are left 2 fend 4 themselves, left all alone.

with the t.vs computers, radios and cd.s some of moral trash.

I wonder if it has a effect, on them the want, the rage, 4 materilstic cash.

the dinner not 2-gether and the remote becomes a child best friend.

Is there a price we all pay, in any nation,

Community Services we must defend!

The kids can't read and the Teachers are blamed 4 the mess.

Isn't that Our responsibility as a Parent 2 Teach and 2 address.

Little Lisa is pregnant and sex is shown on t.v 2 be quite cool.

Isn't there a price all of us pay daily when lust

is promoted in the cultural pool?

Babies having babies and Dad refuses 2 pay child support for all to Win.

A battle where the Children suffer the most,

court t.v promoting conflict, again.

When we loose are values as a nation and the kids are left 2 fend.

Don't we all as a nation suffer the effects from Parenting quite pretend.

Children are not a check in the mail, but a GIFT

from GOD, 4 a Community 2 raise.

And Parenting 4 a Purpose is a Tool, Vital 4 the

Culture, 4 a reason of which 2 Praise.

The parents fight over the basics and Little Johnny

is being bought with possesions.

Isn't Our most Imporatant Job Responisiblity,

Teaching Life long moral lessons?

I am not whining or complaining, just a reality thought 4-2day.

Isn't our most Imporatant Job Parenting each and everday.

2 turn off the t.v and listen, really listen. with all Our Heart.

Isn't that Vital 2 our nation when we all accept,

our individual and National part.

There is no amout of riches that could replace a Childs, Loving smile.

A Lifetime of Teaching Moral values that will

last, the everchanging, Living trial.

A point 2 ponder as many rush 2 work and leave the children alone.

Isn't having a Child about Sacrifice and Structure in the Living zone.

We may blame everyone else but it really comes

down 2 Quality Time 4 sure.

The Time spent Teaching values is Priceless, 4 All of

the Culture a National Foundation a Cure.

By a smaller house don't over spend and Thank GOD everdyay.

4 Children are a Gift, not a check or a fee, and that's cool and quite okay.

Some will say my job isn't Important... I say it's Vital 2 All of our Society.

4 when you spent Time 2 Teach, Everyones Child....

it's called Moral Accountiblity.

Child care at work more affordable, Appreciation

of a Gift, could bring the Children back.

4 as a Nation they are the Future, Leaders a

little TRUTH on the cultural track.

2 Love anyones Child and 2 Sacrifice, a little Time 2 Teach.

Is a Miracle 4 Sure they could be the next

President or Seek 2 Univeraslly,Preach.

When we all Sacrifice 4 another, aren't we really

doing what GOD intended, 4 All.

4 when no-ones there 2 raise the Children as a nation we All, take the fall.

There is no price you can put on a Child, none

4 they are a GOD-Given... Gift.

And it takes a whole nation 2-gether, 2 raise One, not 2 set them adrift.

Vital 2 Our culture.... Vital 2 Our nation.... as

a whole, Universally, and within.

4 when the Youth are put before wealth, All of Our Society, shall Win !!!

SEA OF TOMORROW....

Shed no Tears, Child, no tears of sorrow.

Just look 4 me, in the sea of Tomorrow.

Shed no tears of despair or remorse..

Look 2 the sky....of the Almighty force.

See not my passing as a loss.

Look 2 the Son, or Daughter, on the Cross.

fret not or worry, despair is not allowed.

Look 2 the sea, the stars, and the cloud.

morn not the passing or the death.

Look 2 the Spirit, the Spirit that is left.

Given as a Gift, 2 All of the Children in the sea.

That Believe in the Spirit, the Spirit....of Eternity.

Speak not of that which left in the wake.

Seek 2 Focus, on HOPE..... 2 Give instead of take.

See not the passing in the sea of Tommorow.

But that of JOY, not tears or sorrow.

seek not the materilistic possessions.

Learn 2 Focus in the sea of many lessons.

4 the Gift is not 2 wallow in despair.

But 2 seek, in the Eternal Bliss..... of that still there.

4 the seeds shall bloom, as the stars shall shine.

4 the Gift is Love, seek 2 be kind.

4-give, Learn, let go, and most of All Child, Believe.

4 within the sea of FAITH, there's much 2 Achieve.

Not of Earthly materilstic clout, per say.

But the Gift of Grace, the Gift 2 stay.

4 the Spirit, is alive and beating within All.

4 the Glory of GOD, is 2 listen 4 the call.

Angels in the Mist, Angels.... in the storm.

4 I shall walk once again, in a Child reborn.

Never 2 fade, or wash into the sea.

4 the sea of Tommorow, carries, 4 Eternity.

In the wave of Life, and the valley of the Eternal Bliss.

My life was Blessing in the sea of a Angels Gentle Kiss.

4 the Heartbeat shall carry as the Love shall shine on, my Child.

In the field of Life....where dreams, of HOPE.... grow wild.

the Gift 2 Believe, is a seed in the Heavenly sea.

That opens the Holy door.... which leads, 2 Eternity !!!!

God ...is the calm, after the storm.

The sparkle in the eyes, of a child reborn.

God...is the star twinkling, in the sky.

the hand that wipes the tears, when you cry.

God...is in the tear, after a friends loss.

In the Hope, when you kneel, at the cross.

God is the Comfort, after a friends death.

in the wave of the life, where a memory, is left.

God is in the wind, the breaks the spell, of stifling,heat.

God is the friend...who helps you back, on your feet.

God is in the Hands...U can not see.

The Ones that made, the dogwood tree.

God is the LIght...where we look, straight ahead.

Thankful 4 all, the suffering and the nourishing, Bread.

4 GOD...is everywhere...when you carry, belief.

4 the mind is Clear...FILLED, of Joy, not grief.

from the Long Suffering and Trials...keep this in mind.

4 after the storm...a rainbow, you can find.

4 within GOD... there isn't room, 4 the seed, of doubt.

Faith is the Anchor, as Hope... is the clout.

4 God is there Always... when times, seem bleak.

The Gentle Whisper, in the wind...Comfort 2 speak.

4 God is in the teardrop...you needed, 2 cry.

In the vibrant hawk circling, in the misty, sky.

4 God, is in Charity...without a boasting name.

Anonymous the deed, Humble is the flame.

GOD is in the death...of an only, child.

In the seed of Hope...where Faith, is filed.

GOD is the grandaughter...who cares enough.

2 make the time, 4 grandad's silly stuff.

Who sees not the age, outcome, or falling child.

but the little boy, or girl...within, where Fallin memories, grow wild.

God is in ALL...from the cloud, 2 the sandy shore.

But it's up 2 you...2 open God's door.

that which surrounds, the Heart, Mind and Soul.

GOD is the Comfort... in a storm, windy, bitter, cold.

4 God is in the neighbor...who shares, a warm meal.

GOD is the ability...4 the Heart.... 2 feel.

Never say never...4 the seed, of Priceless Hope.

Can keep the mind... content, down life's, rocky slope

4 when you Believe, ...and graciuosly, give your Heart... 2 God.

in the little treasures, of life...you see, the Heavenly nod.

vivid are the colors, fragrant is now, the rose.

where a heart, was dead... when Faith.... was froze.

4 GOD...is the Hands, that carry, the weight.

2 clear the worries...off Lifes.... plate.